THE HOW AND WHY WONDER® BOOK OF
DINOSAURS

By Darlene Geis

Illustrated by Kenyon Shannon

Edited under the supervision of
Dr. Paul E. Blackwood
Washington, D. C.

Text and illustrations approved by

Oakes A. White
Brooklyn Children's Museum
Brooklyn, New York

PRICE STERN SLOAN
Los Angeles

INTRODUCTION

This book is one in a series of *How and Why Wonder Books* planned to stimulate young readers to explore different areas of science. It dips into the past to tell the real and very exciting story of dinosaurs, a now-extinct group of the reptile family. Children and parents who read this book will soon discover that some of the new things about the old earth are as fascinating as some of the most recent discoveries about space. For, as we read here: "Though the dinosaurs themselves are very old, the science that tells us about them is quite new. And while we have been learning new things about outer space and planets and preparing for the new space age to come, we have also been discovering new things about this old earth and what it was like millions of years ago."

The way scientists have studied the past to learn how dinosaurs looked, how they lived, and how they died is scientific investigation at its best. Piece by piece, they have built skeletons of dinosaurs from real bones. And from a study of geological and fossil evidence, they have figured out the habits of dinosaurs. The investigations have drawn on imagination and careful thinking. Here, as in all science, men have tested their ideas and hunches against all available evidence. If some of our present ideas do not stand the test of new evidence, the ideas will be changed. For that is how scientists work. That is how knowledge grows.

Aside from the fascinating descriptions of *Allosaurus, Brontosaurus, Brachiosaurus* and their countless cousins, this book about dinosaurs gives the reader a tremendous feeling about the great sweep of time and life on our earth. It shows us that the past and the future are both subject to exploration by scientists. The reader cannot help but feel a part of that great exploration.

Paul E. Blackwood

Dr. Blackwood is a professional employee in the U. S. Office of Education. This book was edited by him in his private capacity and no official support or endorsement by the Office of Education is intended or should be inferred.

PART ONE

BURIED TREASURE

How did we first find out about dinosaurs?

ONE DAY, nearly one hundred years ago, some workmen were digging a foundation for a building in a little town in New Jersey. As they dug deeper and deeper into the dirt and rock, they came across what seemed to be huge bones and teeth. The bones and teeth were so hard that they looked as if they had turned into stone.

"Very strange," the workers said as they examined these giant bones. "Too big for a cow or a horse. They're even too big for an elephant!"

The workmen tossed the bones aside and got on with their job of digging. But some of the men brought a few of the strange bones home as curious souvenirs. People in the neighborhood heard about them, and they came by where the men were digging to get a souvenir, too. Those enormous teeth made interesting paperweights, and the big stony bones were heavy enough to use as doorstops.

People digging at construction sites have often found dinosaur bones and teeth.

Were there dinosaurs in the United States?

But finally a famous scientist in nearby Philadelphia heard about these giant bones. He hurried down to get the rest of them, because he had a very exciting thought. Only recently, in England, scientists had discovered some very large and very old skeleton remains of giant animals. After much study they had called the animals "dinosaurs." This is a name they made up from two Greek words meaning "terrible lizards."

Dr. Leidy, the Philadelphia scientist, had a feeling that the bones dug up by the New Jersey workmen were dinosaur bones, too. After many months, Dr. Leidy put the bones together. But he found that many parts were missing.

Back to New Jersey he went, searching from house to house to see if anyone had interesting paperweights, or doorstops or other souvenirs from the digging. People were helpful about giving them up or selling them when they learned why the scientist needed the old bones.

At last Dr. Leidy fitted together a giant skeleton. This proved to be the skeleton of a duck-billed dinosaur. It was the very first dinosaur skeleton found in the United States. And it still stands today in the Philadelphia Academy of Natural Sciences.

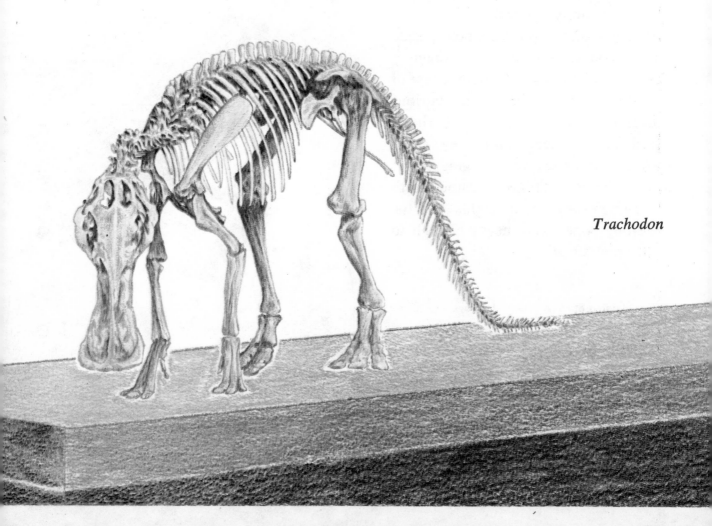

Trachodon

OUR SKELETON ZOOS

How long ago did the dinosaurs live?

SINCE that time, almost a hundred years ago, there have been hundreds of dinosaur skeletons dug up in various parts of the United States. And in many of our cities there are museums where you can see these "skeleton zoos" of animals that lived millions and millions of years ago. Dinosaurs lived on this earth 200 million years ago, to be exact.

When you go to one of these museums and look up at the giant beasts towering over you, you can be very glad that they lived so many millions of years ago!

Were there people living in the time of the dinosaurs?

As a matter of fact, dinosaurs lived and died out long, long before the first man appeared on earth. And it's amazing to think that only human beings living in the past hundred years or so have even known or seen what a dinosaur looked like! Though the dinosaurs themselves are so very, very old, the science that tells us about them is quite new. And while we have been learning new things about outer space and planets and preparing for the new space age to come, we have also been discovering new things about this old earth and what it was like millions of years ago.

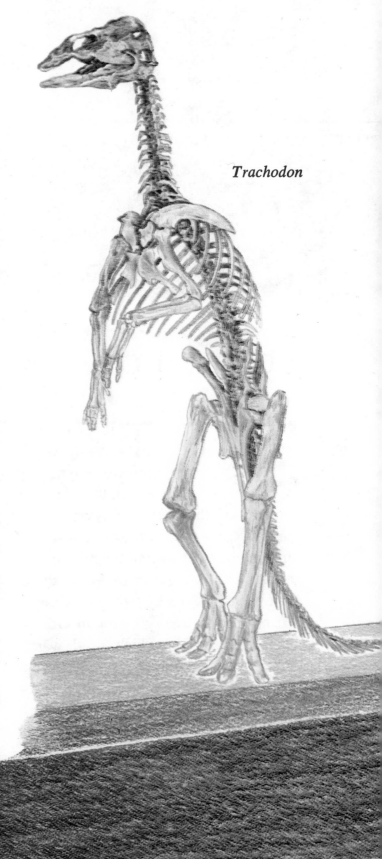

Trachodon

LONG, LONG AGO

What was the earth like when dinosaurs lived on it?

THE EARTH was very different when the dinosaurs were living on it. In the first place, it was warm everywhere — and all of the time. Imagine summer lasting for millions of years all over the world! Why, there were even palm trees growing in Alaska! There were fig trees growing in Greenland. And corals, which need warm water, were building reefs 'way up on the Canadian shores.

Though there were some mountains and volcanoes, most of the land was low and flat. Warm seas flooded over much of what is land today. And there were marshes and swamps, thick with green plants. There were many shallow lagoons with water plants growing in them. Swamp forests like the Everglades in Florida grew dense and green. And on the plains there were scattered trees that looked like giant ferns. We know that it must have rained a lot to keep everything so green and moist.

How did life on earth begin?

In the beginning there had been life only in the seas. That is where life first started. There were all kinds of shell creatures and corals and sea animals that looked like flowers. Then the seas began to swarm with fish, some of them enormous. And some of the fish, after millions of years, became able to live part of the time on land. They began to look less like fish as they developed little legs.

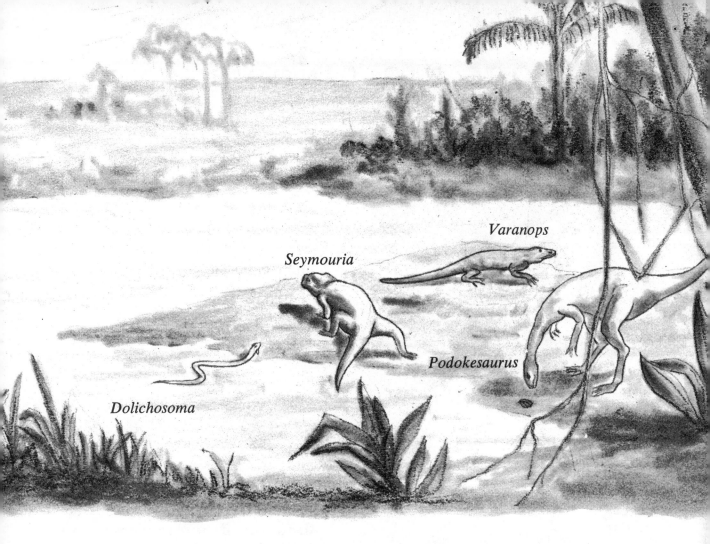

Varanops

Seymouria

Podokesaurus

Dolichosoma

Finally some of these creatures became able to live on land all of the time. They were able to lay their eggs on land, too. These first completely land-living animals were called "reptiles," which means "those who crawl." There were many different reptile families. There were the turtles, the snakes and the lizards. And there was also the reptile family which included the dinosaurs.

How long did the dinosaurs last? The dinosaurs ruled this warm, moist and summery world for more than one hundred million years. "One hundred million years" might not sound like much when you say it fast, but stop and think about it a moment. That is *one hundred times longer than the whole time that man has been on earth.* You have to stretch your imagination quite a bit even to get the idea. There's one thing about dinosaurs, though, if you're going to think about them at all: think BIG!

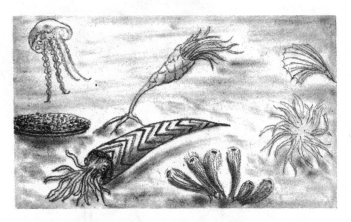

MANY EARLY SEA ANIMALS RESEMBLED FLOWERS.

Tyrannosaurus rex

Pteranodon

Triceratops

Camptosaurus

Stegosaurus

How did dinosaurs get their names?

ONE of the BIG things about dinosaurs is their names. Now there's a reason — a good reason — for these long tongue-twisters. Scientists name all plants and animals by putting together Latin and Greek words that tell something about the plant or animal. That becomes the scientific name for it in all countries, whatever their language. So scientists all over the world understand one another when it comes to scientific names.

When you learn the names of these dinosaurs, you can be sure that boys and girls in France or Russia or Germany or South America are calling them by the very same names. Take the dinosaur, *Brontosaurus* (bron-tuh-SOR-us), for example. That means "thunder lizard." And now that you understand it, you will find it as easy to rattle off as "hippopotamus" (which means "river horse," by the way).

Each time you see a dinosaur name, remember that it usually means something simple that describes the animal. Consult the glossary on page 48 for a complete list of the names of dinosaurs and other prehistoric animals that are used in this book.

Now let's step into the world of the dinosaurs and learn their story.

Diplodocus

Kannemeyeria

Saltoposuchus

Phytosaur

Dimetrodon

Ornithopoda

PART TWO

THE FIRST DINOSAURS

Are all dinosaurs big?

DINOSAURS did not just suddenly appear on earth. They developed slowly from one of the reptile families during the great Age of Reptiles. At first they were small creatures not more than two or three feet long. They were cold-blooded like the other reptiles, but instead of crawling along the ground on four legs, the early dinosaurs scampered along on their hind legs. Their small front legs had clawlike hands, and they balanced themselves by means of a long, skinny, lizard-like tail.

Though these early dinosaurs were small, they were fierce. They were meat-eaters who fed on other small reptiles. Because of their speed, and because they used their front legs for grasping and tearing their prey, they had a big advantage. Their small four-legged neighbors didn't stand a chance against them.

What did dinosaurs eat?

So the dinosaurs thrived. Some of them grew larger and continued to scurry through the leafy green plants hunting down other animals. These meat-eaters, no matter how large they grew, always walked on their powerful hind legs. Their forelegs remained like tiny arms held close to their chest.

But some of the early dinosaurs developed differently. Over many, many years, they lived on a rich diet of plants. The world was carpeted with juicy green leaves, and a plant-eating animal could spend its whole life just in eating. By and by, some of these plant-eaters grew to enormous size.

Were all dinosaurs meat-eaters?

Finally, the plant-eating dinosaurs had to drop down to a four-legged position. In the first place, it was easier to reach the plants that way. In the second place, they were getting too heavy to support their weight on two legs. As a matter of fact, it wasn't always easy to carry all those pounds around on four legs! So some of the largest plant-eaters spent a lot of time in the water. This helped them hold up their weight, because their great bodies could float partly in the water.

Tyrannosaurus re.
(Cretaceous Period)

Brontosaurus
(Jurassic Period)

Did dinosaurs live on land or in the water?

Also, when the gentle plant-eaters were in the water, they were safe from their fierce two-legged, meat-eating cousins. The two-legged dinosaurs didn't dare to do more than get their big hind feet wet, even when they saw a delicious dinosaur dinner just a little way out in the lake. And that was a lucky thing for the plant-eaters. Since they were slow and clumsy, and did not have sharp teeth or claws or any other weapons, the lakes and lagoons were all that saved them from the terrible hunters on land.

What is the balance of nature? In all groups of animals that live side by side in the world, there have to be some who hunt and some who are the hunted. There must be some who eat plants and some who eat flesh. This is called the balance of nature. If all animals were plant-eaters, there would soon be too many of them. They would eat the world bare, and there would not be enough food for all. By having some animals feed on other animals, their number is kept down, and there is a balance between the kinds of animals and their food. In that way there is a chance for many kinds of life, both plant and animal, to thrive on earth.

All animals develop, for the most part, according to their eating habits. This is true among our groups of animals today, and you will see that it was true millions of years ago among the different dinosaur groups, too.

THE DINOSAUR GIANTS

AFTER the dinosaurs had been developing for millions of years, some of them grew to be tremendous in size. The climate was just right for them — warm and moist and comfortable for cold-blooded reptiles. Reptiles can be active only in warm climates.

The great plains were jungles of juicy green plants. Shallow pools and lakes and marshes had clumps of green in them. So some dinosaurs could feed even in the water.

The dinosaurs chewed and munched and thumped across the land, kings of the whole green world. And the world would have been a dinosaur heaven if it weren't for a terrible creature named *Allosaurus*.

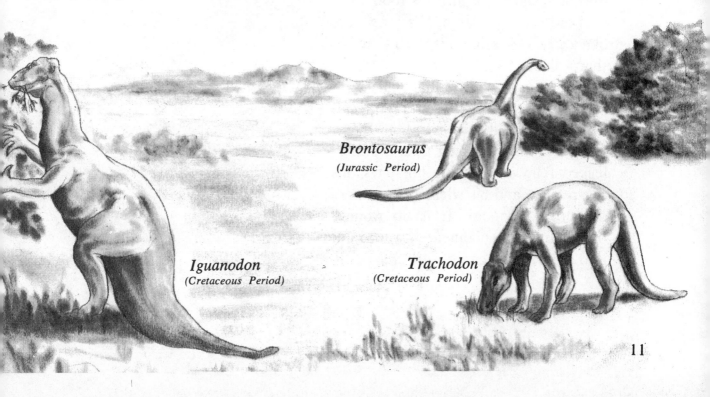

Iguanodon
(Cretaceous Period)

Brontosaurus
(Jurassic Period)

Trachodon
(Cretaceous Period)

ALLOSAURUS

(al-uh-SOR-us)

Which was one of the fiercest dinosaurs? THE NAME *Allosaurus* comes from two Greek words meaning "other lizard." It is a rather tame name for such a fierce beast. He was a giant meat-eating dinosaur who lived on the other giant dinosaurs of his time.

There were other, smaller meat-eaters who fed on the smaller dinosaurs. But *Allosaurus,* because of his size, was the most terrible of all. He was 35 feet long from the tip of his big tail to the front of his huge jaws!

Allosaurus had strong, heavy hind legs on which he ran. His hind feet had three clawed toes, rather like a bird's. The long tail helped him balance on two legs, like a seesaw. Up in front were two tiny arms with heavy curved claws that he could hook into his food. And his head was very large. His jaws were like a crocodile's, and his teeth were big sharp blades.

Though some of the plant-eating dinosaurs were much bigger than *Allosaurus,* they could not fight him. In the first place, he was faster than the four-legged fellows. And his big jaws, his sharp teeth, and his wicked claws were dangerous weapons. It is no wonder that many of the plant-eaters waded out into the water to escape *Allosaurus.*

How could the other dinosaurs defend themselves? Other plant-eaters developed a kind of bony armor that helped protect them. But we can imagine that when *Allosaurus* came bounding across the green and pleasant land, looking for his dinner, none of the other dinosaurs were really safe.

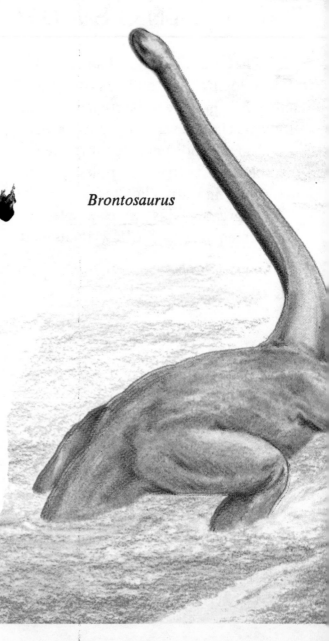

Brontosaurus

Allosaurus

Brontosaurus

BRONTOSAURUS

(bron-tuh-SOR-us)

What does Brontosaurus mean?

BRONTOSAURUS means "thunder lizard." The scientist who named him had a good imagination. He must have thought: "The ground probably shook and thundered every time this giant took a heavy step, so I'll call him 'thunder lizard.'"

Skeletons of *Brontosaurus* have been found right here in North America. When the scientists put the first one together, they must have been surprised! For there they saw an animal measuring 70 feet long. It had a heavy tail that seemed to go on and on until it tapered off to a long thin point. Its body must have been the size of a small blimp. And four stout legs like tree trunks held it up. Then a long neck, almost as long as the tail, stretched out in front.

But strangest of all was the small head, no bigger around than the neck. And the mouth that fed that whole enormous animal was quite small. In it there were about twenty-four weak, peg-shaped teeth.

Brontosaurus, the scientists decided, must have kept that little mouth busy munching plants nearly every minute. Otherwise he could never have taken in enough food to feed his huge body.

How big was Brontosaurus?

Though *Brontosaurus* could thump around on land, nibbling at the plants that grew there, he probably was never far from the water. And he spent a good part of his time in the water, which helped support his weight. No wonder! This dinosaur weighed 60,000 pounds! He was as large as seven big elephants!

When his terrible enemy, *Allosaurus,* came in sight, *Brontosaurus* would move out into deeper water. He could go out pretty far and still keep his head well above water. He did not even have to stop eating.

But sometimes *Brontosaurus* was up on dry land near the shore when *Allosaurus* came hunting for meat. Then there was only one thing to do. *Brontosaurus* would have to turn tail and move — as fast as his size would let him — to the safety of the lake. Maybe at those moments he was able to use his long tail like a whip and strike it against the head of the enemy that was chasing him.

How do we know how dinosaurs hunted? At the American Museum of Natural History in New York City, you can see the record of just such a chase. It was printed in the mud (now turned to sandstone) by the dinosaurs' feet 120 million years ago. There are the big basin-shaped footprints of *Brontosaurus*. And farther back, in among the larger footprints, are the three-pointed, birdlike prints of *Allosaurus*. In a few places *Allosaurus* had even stepped into the holes made by the big feet of *Brontosaurus*. He had certainly been hot on his trail on that bygone day.

But did he catch him? Was *Brontosaurus* eaten then and there? Or did the big peaceful fellow get into the water in the nick of time? Well, sometimes he was safe and sometimes he wasn't. In this case we will never know.

BRACHIOSAURUS

(brak-ee-uh-SOR-us)

Which was the heaviest dinosaur of all? THE GREEK words meaning "arm lizard" give this giant of giants his name. The bones of his forearm were unusually large, and that is why he was called "arm lizard."

Brachiosaurus was the biggest and heaviest of all the dinosaurs. He was so tall that his little head could easily have looked over a three-story building. Most dinosaurs had longer hind legs than forelegs, but this one was built differently. His long neck went straight up, too. And there was a reason for this dinosaur's great height.

Brachiosaurus was so heavy — he weighed 100,000 pounds — that he could barely drag himself around on land. So he couldn't fight or run away from his enemies. Therefore, he spent nearly all of his time in the water. He was able to go out into very deep water and still keep his head above the surface. That was where the long neck and long front legs were a help.

How could a dinosaur breathe under water? There was something else that was unusual about this biggest dinosaur. At the very top of his head he had a dome with nostrils in it. *Brachiosaurus* could stay hidden under water with just this little breathing dome showing.

There were plenty of water plants for him to feed on. And this great clumsy creature spent most of his time standing in the water, chewing on plants. He couldn't move around much on land. He couldn't swim in the water. It must have been a dull way to live— even for a dinosaur.

Brachiosaurus

DIPLODOCUS

(dih-PLOD-uh-kuss)

Which was the longest dinosaur of all?

DIPLODO-CUS got his name from the two Greek words meaning "double beam." Take one look at him and you'll know why. He had a body with two long beams sticking out — one in front and one in back. And it wasn't very easy to tell which beam had the brain.

Like the other big plant-eating dinosaurs who waded in the swamps and lakes, *Diplodocus* had a very small head. Scientists are puzzled about how that tiny mouth and narrow neck could let him get enough food down to feed his big body. *Diplodocus* was the longest of the dinosaurs, but he was lighter and thinner than his big relatives. He was 87½ feet long. That's about as long as seven automobiles standing bumper to bumper! It took a lot of food to fill up an animal that size.

Diplodocus

How could some big dinosaurs hide themselves? *Diplodocus* spent most of his time in the water, too. His nostrils and eyes were high up on his small head. He could keep himself well hidden under water, and his long neck could stretch way up, letting him just breathe and see. He wasn't very smart, but he knew how to hide from his enemies.

All the big, slow, wading dinosaurs were probably the first to die out. They needed low swampy land and the kind of soft plants that grew there and in the water. Their teeth weren't strong enough to chew the tougher dry plants.

After many millions of years, when the shallow water began to drain away, these gentle giants were no longer able to live on the drier land. Even if they could have gotten along on a diet of different plants, they still would have needed the swamps and lakes to hide in. If they could not plunge into water, there was no other way for them to escape meat-eating *Allosaurus*.

STEGOSAURUS

(steg-uh-SOR-us)

Why did some dinosaurs have armor?

THE "cover lizard" was covered with armor and bony plates. That's how he got his name. If you can picture a tank walking, that's *Stegosaurus!* But he was not a tank that attacked other animals. He ate plants, and his armor was just to protect him from the meat-eating dinosaurs who might have tried to eat him.

Could plant-eating dinosaurs fight?

When you look at a picture of *Stegosaurus,* the first thing you notice is the double row of heavy bone-plates on his back. They reach from just behind his head almost to the tip of his tail. That tail had four sharp, strong spikes sprouting from it. *Stegosaurus* couldn't move very fast, but he could swat that spiked tail back and forth. Any enemy getting hit by that weapon would soon leave *Stegosaurus* alone. And that is exactly what *Stegosaurus* wanted.

Another odd thing about *Stegosaurus* was the length of his hind legs and the shortness of his front ones. It is easy to see that once he had an ancestor who walked on strong hind legs.

But *Stegosaurus,* walking on all fours, had his hips high in the air and his head close to the ground. He could nibble at low plants easily, but he must have moved very clumsily.

How big was the brain of a dinosaur?

And to finish the picture of this odd-looking dinosaur, there was his tiny head. It was a small head for such a large animal. The brain of *Stegosaurus* was just about the size of a walnut, only large enough to work his jaws and front legs. Back near his hips was a place in his spine twenty times larger than his brain, a "second brain" that worked his big hind legs and his tail.

In spite of his small brain, *Stegosaurus* was an improvement over earlier dinosaurs. He came along a little later than they did, though they all lived side by side for a long time. *Stegosaurus* could grind and crush the harder, drier plants that grew up on higher, drier land. And his armor and tail gave him some protection from his fierce meat-eating enemies.

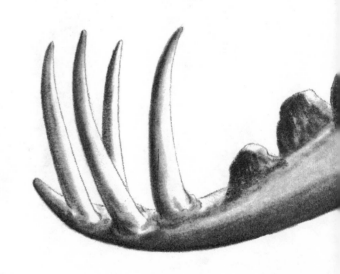

Stegosaurus

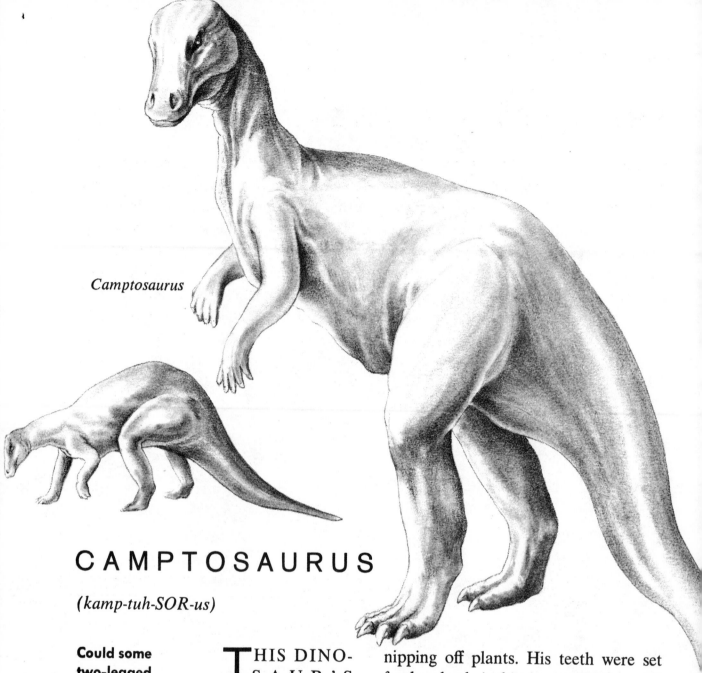

Camptosaurus

CAMPTOSAURUS

(kamp-tuh-SOR-us)

Could some two-legged dinosaurs walk on all fours?

THIS DINO- SAUR'S name means "bent" or "flexible lizard." He was called that because he could walk on his big hind legs, or he could bend down and walk on all fours.

Camptosaurus ate plants. He was the grandfather of a whole new group of plant-eating dinosaurs that were to come later, in the second great age of dinosaurs. He had a horny beak at the front of his mouth, and he used it for nipping off plants. His teeth were set further back in his jaws, and he used them to grind up his food.

This dinosaur was not very large. He could move around more easily than the clumsy giants, but he had no armor and no weapons, and he probably couldn't escape from his enemies in deep water. *Camptosaurus* must have made a fine meal for *Allosaurus,* the terrible hunter. But the great-great-grandchildren of *Camptosaurus,* who came later, were sometimes able to escape from the hunting beasts, as we shall see.

PART THREE

THE LAST OF THE DINOSAURS

**Were there
two groups
of dinosaurs?**

DINO-SAURS had been the most important animals on earth for seventy million years. The plant-eaters had become giants, as we have seen, because there were so many rich green plants growing in their swamps. And the hunters grew great, too, because there was so much meat for them.

There were changes on the earth.

For the first time flowers appeared. And there were tree-oaks, willows and palms. And a different group of dinosaurs lived on this flowering land. None of the new dinosaurs ever became as huge as the old giants, but they were big enough! And many of them were the strangest looking dinosaurs of all.

This last great age of dinosaurs went on for fifty million years more. And then the great beasts that had ruled the world for such a long time died out.

Allosaurus
(Jurassic Period)

Stegosaurus
(Jurassic Period)

Triceratops
(Cretaceous Period)

Styracosaurus
(Cretaceous Period)

Ankylosaurus
(Cretaceous Period)

Trachodon

TRACHODON

(TRAK-uh-don)

Could some dinosaurs swim?

TRACHODON means "rough-toothed." This dinosaur got his name because he had two thousand teeth in his large mouth. His teeth were for grinding, not for biting, and he was a gentle plant-eater. Another nickname for this dinosaur and his relatives is "duck-billed dinosaur," and if you look at his picture you will see why.

The duck-bills were the great-great-grandchildren of *Camptosaurus. Trachodon* looked a lot like his grandfather, except that he was larger. His head had flattened and spread into a broad bill, like a duck's. And his feet had become webbed — also like a duck's.

Trachodon must have spent most of his time in the water. His heavy tail and webbed feet would have helped him swim well. And his duck-bill would have been a good shovel for digging plants out of the mud.

This is the kind of dinosaur that was the first one found in the United States. Remember Dr. Joseph Leidy who collected some of the old bones from souvenir hunters? Imagine trying to put together a dinosaur skeleton with two thousand teeth!

Some other duck-billed dinosaurs developed strange humps of bone on their skulls. And some of them grew long tubes of bone on top of their heads. These seemed to be used for breathing under water, and they were a little like the snorkels that skin-divers use today.

The only way these duck-billed dinosaurs could escape from the dreadful meat-eating monsters was to get into the water and stay there. So they developed webbed feet and duck-bills and special ways of breathing in the water. That way they were able to get along quite well without having to spend much time up on land where the dangerous hunters lived.

ANKYLOSAURUS

(an-kil-uh-SOR-us)

Did their armor help the dinosaurs? THIS "curved lizard" got his name because of the way his ribs curved heavily over his back. He was an example of another way the plant-eaters could defend themselves against the meat-eaters. *Ankylosaurus* wore armor. He was the walking tank of his time, just as *Stegosaurus* had been at an earlier time.

Ankylosaurus did not have to live near the water for safety, as his other relatives did. As a matter of fact, he would have sunk like a stone if he had ever tried hiding in the water! This armored dinosaur was quite safe from *Tyrannosaurus rex* (ty-ran-uh-SOR-us rex) or the other meat-eaters. Even their sharp teeth and claws could not get at *his* meat. It was locked in bone.

The back of *Ankylosaurus* was covered with bony plates that protected him. They curved over him like a turtle's shell. Then he had long spikes that stuck out from the sides of his body and protected his short legs. Even his head had a bony covering, which served as a kind of helmet.

Most useful of all was the marvelous tail of this armored dinosaur. It was covered with rings of bone. At the end of the tough, hard tail was a great lump of bone. Any meat-eater who tried to eat this dinosaur would get a strong whack from that heavy tail. It was enough to send the hunter away to look for an easier meal.

Why were there so many kinds of dinosaurs? These dinosaurs lived on the higher dry land, away from the swamps and marshes. You can see that every kind of dinosaur had his own favorite place to live. There would have been no balance of life if they all wanted to live in the water, or if they all wanted to live up on dry land. So each found his own best place, and after millions of years their bodies changed to fit their kind of life.

In that way there was enough room and enough food for everyone. And because of their different lives they developed into many different kinds of creatures.

Ankylosaurus

Protoceratops

PROTOCERATOPS

(proh-toh-SER-uh-tops)

THIS long name comes from three Greek words that mean "first horn-face." When you look at this dinosaur's picture, you may wonder who ever decided to call him "horn-face," because he had no horns on his face.

Well, *Protoceratops* was the first of a large family of horn-faced dinosaurs. But he himself never had any horns. He was also the smallest of the family, as he grew only to about five or six feet in length.

Protoceratops and his family were the last of the dinosaurs to appear on earth. They were plant-eaters and quite remarkable looking. *Protoceratops* walked on four short legs, close to the ground. He had a body like a lizard's and an unusual head. His head was large and it began with a beak like a parrot's. Then it humped up near the nose. There was a big bony collar, or frill, that curved back over his neck and shoulders.

In the great-grandchildren of *Protoceratops* the hump would become a horn. And the bony collar would grow larger on the great-grandchildren, and sometimes it would even have spikes on it. These dinosaurs developed horns and spikes as a defense against the fierce hunters who lived when they did.

Did dinosaurs lay eggs? Scientists have found out a lot about *Protoceratops*. It is the only dinosaur whose eggs have ever been discovered. And so many skeletons of "first horn-face" have been dug up that scientists have very young ones and full-grown ones in their museums. So scientists can study the growth of this dinosaur from a baby to a grownup.

The new-hatched *Protoceratops* had no bony frill on his small skull, but as he grew larger, the frill began to grow. By the time the dinosaur was full-grown, he had a well-covered neck. The back of the neck was a favorite place for meat-eating animals to attack, so you can see that the bony frill of *Protoceratops* was not there just to look pretty. It was really very useful.

Iguanodon

IGUANODON

(ih-GWAN-uh-don)

THIS dinosaur got his name because of a mistake. The scientist who first found some of its large teeth thought that they looked like the teeth of our modern iguanas, only bigger. So he called the creature *Iguanodon*, which means "iguana lizard" and "tooth."

Which was the first dinosaur ever found?

Iguanodon was the first giant reptile to be described. In fact, the word "dinosaur" had not even been invented at the time. In addition to the teeth, a few of his big bones were found in a rock quarry in England. After much puzzling, the scientist who found them decided they did not belong to any animal that was known.

"This is a new kind of animal entirely," the scientist said. "Some sort of reptile, and a giant one at that." In calling him *Iguanodon,* he named the first dinosaur to be revealed after millions of years.

29

TRICERATOPS

(try-SER-uh-tops)

Which was the last dinosaur to appear on earth?

THIS name means "three-horned face." And if you count the horns in the picture, you will agree that the name is right. Old "three-horns" was the last of the horned dinosaurs, and the greatest of them all.

He was 30 feet long, and a strong fighter. Although *Triceratops* ate plants, he was not a gentle animal. Nature had given him a head full of wonderful fighting weapons. He had his three sharp horns, and a bony shield that protected his head, his neck and his shoulders.

Were any of the plant-eaters fierce?

He was not one to let his weapons go to waste. Some of his bones show so many scars that we know he must have fought off the huge hunters many times.

Triceratops probably charged at his enemies fiercely, the way our present-day rhinoceros does. His neck muscles were very strong, and his big body and heavy legs had power, too.

When *Triceratops* used his swordlike horns against the dagger teeth of *Tyrannosaurus rex,* the earth must have shaken. That really must have been a championship fight!

Triceratops

Tyrannosaurus rex

32

TYRANNOSAURUS REX

(ty-ran-uh-SOR-us rex)

THE MOST famous of all the dinosaurs was this fierce king of the meat-eaters. His name means "king of the tyrant lizards." A tyrant is a cruel ruler, so he was well-named.

Tyrannosaurus rex was the last of the great meat-eating dinosaurs. He was built very much like the first little dinosaurs. And you can see a close family resemblance between him and *Allosaurus,* who had lived much earlier.

Did the meat-eaters have big teeth?

But *Tyrannosaurus rex* was bigger and more terrible. His head was very large. His jaws were huge, and when they opened wide they were edged with sharp curved teeth. Some of those teeth were six inches long!

The "king of the tyrant lizards" was 45 feet long. When he stood up on his heavy hind legs he was nearly 19 feet tall. His front legs had become so small that they couldn't even reach his head. But *Tyrannosaurus rex* didn't need them. His dreadful jaws and heavy-clawed hind feet were all he needed for attacking the other dinosaurs.

Tyrannosaurus rex was not afraid of any other living creature. His teeth could bite through the toughest hide and crunch the thickest bones. No wonder the other dinosaurs that lived when he did had to hide in the water or protect themselves with armor!

What was it like in the dinosaurs' world? Let us try to imagine what life was like in those long-ago times. There are volcanoes rumbling and smoking in the distance. The air is warm and the earth is green and flowering. The giant monsters that rule the earth move slowly from plant to plant. They spend most of their time eating.

The plant-eating dinosaurs clump heavily on the soft ground. They eat the leaves from the tops of tall trees. Some of them wade in shallow muddy water. Others move out in deeper water, rooting around for juicy plants.

Suddenly there is a disturbance. A few of the smaller, faster dinosaurs scurry by, running on their hind legs. A duck-billed fellow pounds by on his heavy hind legs, leaning forward in his hurry to reach the water quickly.

Triceratops lifts his heavy head and keeps on chewing his leaves. But he is ready to charge in case of danger. Only *Ankylosaurus* stays where he is. He knows he is safe under his curved armor.

And then the cause of all the disturbance appears. *Tyrannosaurus rex* crashes through a grove of young oak trees. He is as tall as some of the trees, and his great jaws are open for attack. He strides across the green ground looking for food.

Could Tyrannosaurus rex eat an armored dinosaur? His wicked little eyes catch sight of *Ankylosaurus*, and he bounds over toward him, snapping his jaws. But the sharp teeth of the "king of the tyrant lizards" cannot bite through the heavy armor of *Ankylosaurus*.

Instead, *Ankylosaurus* swings his club of a tail. There is a sharp crack as it whacks his enemy's jaw. A tooth breaks, and *Tyrannosaurus rex* backs off grunting in pain and anger. This creature is not good to eat!

Tyrannosaurus rex

Ankylosaurus

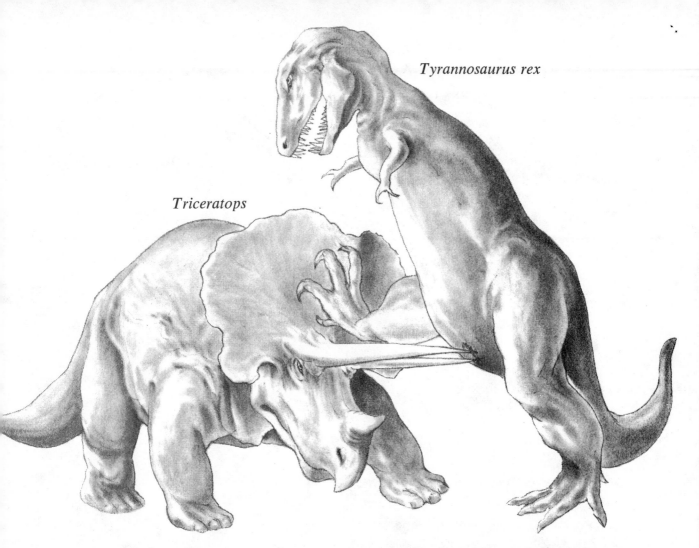

Tyrannosaurus rex

Triceratops

How did dinosaurs fight? Then *Tyrannosaurus rex* sees *Triceratops*. He takes two giant strides and he is almost upon him. But *Triceratops* is a good fighter himself. He lowers his heavy head with its shield of bone and its three sharp horns.

He charges like a rhinoceros at the much bigger *Tyrannosaurus rex*. The earth shakes as these two monsters come together. Every other sound is hushed as the two giants fight it out. *Tyrannosaurus rex* swings his great jaws open and drops down to slash at his foe's back. But *Triceratops* lunges at the soft underside of his enemy.

Both dinosaurs are wounded. *Triceratops* has a deep gash in his back.

But *Tyrannosaurus rex* has been stabbed, and his breath comes in gasps. He cannot turn and run for his life. He must obey his hunger which tells him to get meat in his jaws.

Again *Tyrannosaurus rex* snaps at the backbone of *Triceratops*. And again *Triceratops* charges with his sharp horns. The horns go deep, and the terrible *Tyrannosaurus rex* shudders and kicks as he falls dead to the ground.

But many times it was *Tyrannosaurus rex* who won and feasted on the other dinosaur. This day a lucky *Triceratops* limped away from the battlefield. He carried the scars of his victory for the rest of his life. And millions of years later, in a museum, those scars on his fossil bones tell his story to us.

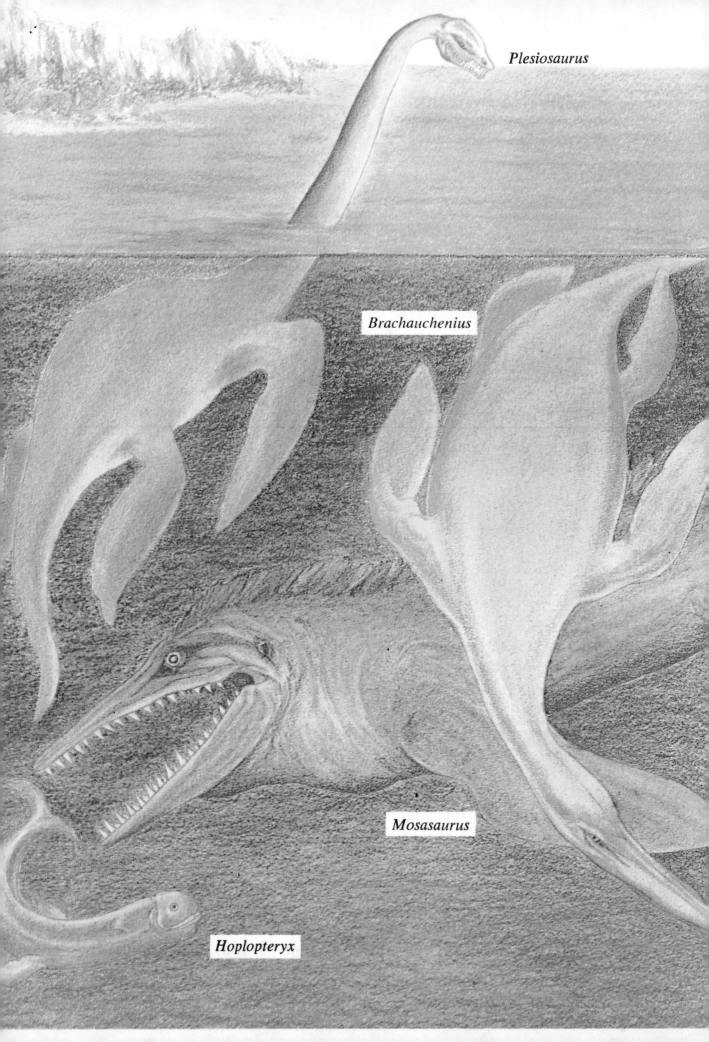

Plesiosaurus

Brachauchenius

Mosasaurus

Hoplopteryx

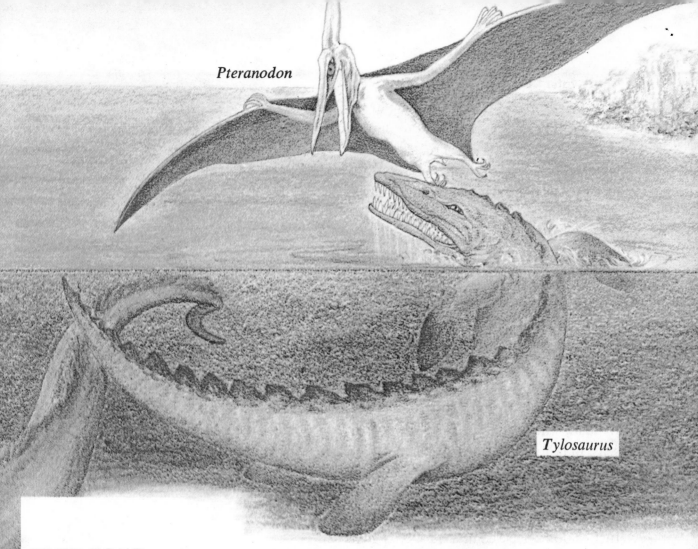

Pteranodon

Tylosaurus

PART FOUR

THE SEA AND AIR REPTILES

Were there flying dinosaurs? And were there dinosaurs that lived in the sea?

NOW WE have met most of the important dinosaurs that lived during the two great dinosaur ages. The world pretty much belonged to them for 120 million years.

During this long time, while the dinosaurs ruled on land, there were some other reptiles that ruled in the sea and in the air. They were not dinosaurs, though they were distantly related, since all of them were reptiles. Some of these creatures became nearly as large and fierce as the big dinosaurs.

You remember that the reptiles were the first creatures capable of living completely on land. Far back at the beginning of reptile history, some reptiles, after living on land and breathing air, moved from the land to the sea. They were still reptiles, but after millions of years their shape and look changed. They had to become more suited for a life in water.

For instance, their reptile legs began to look more like fins or paddles. Legs are fine for land animals, but fins and paddles are better to swim with.

Cladoselache

Were water reptiles meat- or plant-eaters?
The seas were full of fish, but the largest and fiercest sea creatures were water reptiles. Every one of them ate fish rather than sea plants. There was one that looked like a huge fish with flippers, a big tail, and a sharklike fin on its back. This monster had long pointed jaws armed with sharp teeth, and it fed on other fish.

There were giant turtles over 12 feet long. One of them weighed 6,000 pounds! That would make a great deal of turtle soup! But those old king-size turtles had no enemies to worry about. Instead, they swam about in shallow seas, making life dangerous for the poor fish on which they fed.

The turtle family is still living today, but on a much smaller scale. Little turtles don't need as much food as giant ones. So they have a better chance to go on living.

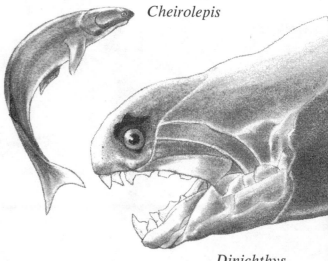
Cheirolepis

Dinichthys

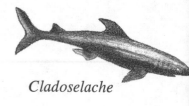
Cladoselache

Pleuracanthus

Archelon

Ichthyosaurus

Eurhinosaurus

Portheus

39

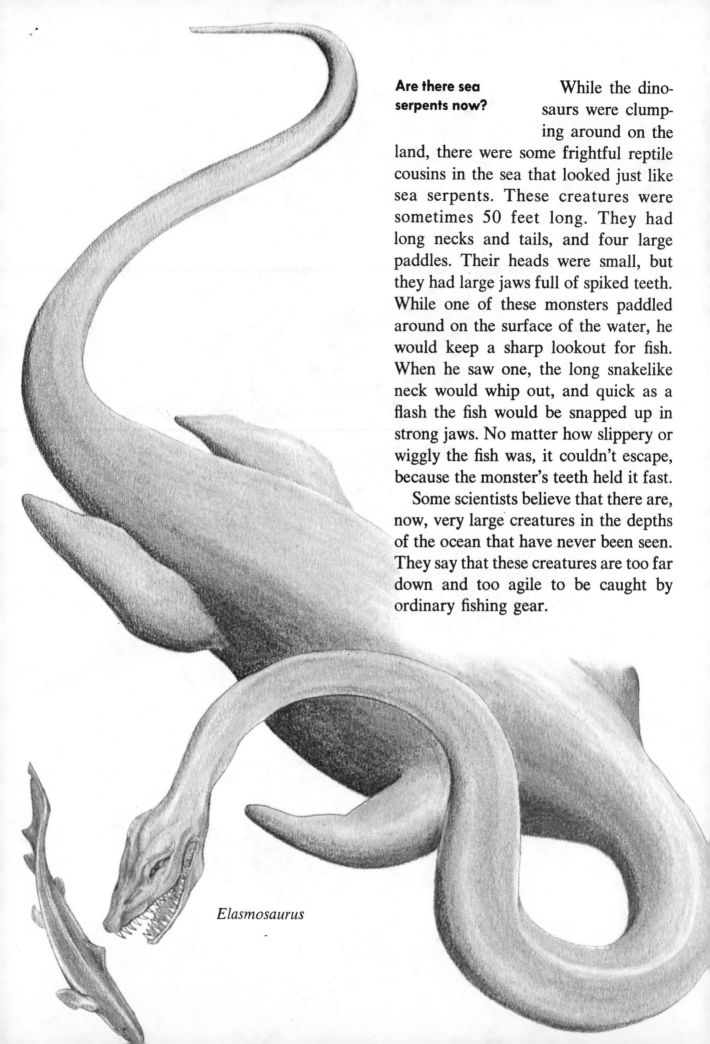

Are there sea serpents now?

While the dinosaurs were clumping around on the land, there were some frightful reptile cousins in the sea that looked just like sea serpents. These creatures were sometimes 50 feet long. They had long necks and tails, and four large paddles. Their heads were small, but they had large jaws full of spiked teeth. While one of these monsters paddled around on the surface of the water, he would keep a sharp lookout for fish. When he saw one, the long snakelike neck would whip out, and quick as a flash the fish would be snapped up in strong jaws. No matter how slippery or wiggly the fish was, it couldn't escape, because the monster's teeth held it fast.

Some scientists believe that there are, now, very large creatures in the depths of the ocean that have never been seen. They say that these creatures are too far down and too agile to be caught by ordinary fishing gear.

Elasmosaurus

Were flying reptiles birds?

Besides the land and the seas being filled with horrible monsters, even the air had dragon-like reptiles flapping through it. These were not true birds, even though they had wings and took to the air.

At first the flying reptiles were small — only about the size of a sparrow. But they were mean-looking little creatures with long jaws full of teeth. They had claws on their wings, and a long bony tail with a fin at the end of it.

Did flying reptiles have feathers?

The later flying reptiles lost their teeth and most of their tail. But they had long pointed beaks, and a big crest of bone at the back of the head. Their wings were like glider wings of skin — these reptiles had no feathers. And the wings had claws on them, too.

The largest of these "flying dragons" was the size of a small airplane. His wingspread was 27 feet! Furthermore, all of these reptiles of the air were meat-eaters. They hunted small animals or fish from the air. Then they swooped down and snapped them up in their long jaws.

The world was a dangerous place in those days. There were "giants" on the earth, "monsters" in the sea, and "dragons" in the air!

Rhamphorhynchus

Pteranodon

Archaeopteryx

Dimorphodon

What happened to the dinosaurs and their relatives?

After being masters of the land, sea and air for 120 million years, most of the reptiles died out rather suddenly. Scientists are still trying to solve the mystery of this great dying. So far, they have discovered some interesting clues, but they are still not sure of the answer.

Titanothere

Patriofelis

Uintatherium

Eohippus

Barylambda

Indricotherium

PART FIVE

WHY DID THE DINOSAURS DISAPPEAR?

Did the dinosaurs' world stay the same?

WHEN the dinosaurs lived on earth, the climate was warm and mild everywhere. Then, very slowly, things began to change. The warm swamps dried up. The air was cooler. New and different kinds of plants began to grow.

There were many animals that were able to get along with these changes, and they didn't die out. But perhaps the dinosaurs could not live in the new kind of world. They were cold-blooded, and they could not live comfortably in cool weather.

The plant-eaters could not eat the new kinds of plants, which had tougher stems and leaves. If the plant-eaters died out because their food had become scarce, you know how that would affect the meat-eaters. They would die out, too, because they had to live on the plant-eaters.

Crocodile

Snake

Turtle

Lizard

Did all reptiles die out at the same time?

The temperature of the seas grew colder, too. And that might have killed off the water reptiles at the same time. But scientists are not completely satisfied with this explanation, because some reptiles managed to live on. Turtles, crocodiles, snakes and lizards are still with us to this day. Why was it just the dinosaurs and other reptile giants that couldn't live on?

What happened to many of the dinosaur eggs? Another explanation is the story of what happened to the dinosaurs' eggs. The big beasts laid their giant eggs right on the ground. They didn't hide them, or protect them, or stay nearby to guard them. When the eggs hatched, the baby dinosaurs had to look after themselves. Other animals, including some of the smaller meat-eating dinosaurs, would get at the unprotected eggs. They made a fine, safe meal for a hungry little animal that had to hide from the big dinosaurs most of the time.

Many dinosaur eggs were surely destroyed in this way. But that alone could not have caused the whole dinosaur family to die out. The big sea reptiles died out at the same time, and their young were born alive in the water. So egg robbers cannot have been to blame completely.

Another idea is that there was a special kind of dinosaur sickness that killed the giants. Scientists wonder if there might not have been a disease that spread all over the world, affecting only dinosaurs and the big air and water reptiles. But then, why did it skip other reptiles?

Maybe the answer is a combination of all of these ideas. And maybe the warm-blooded furry mammals had something to do with it. They were a new kind of animal and had developed while the great dinosaurs ruled. They were small and not important at first.

Amebelodon

Smilodon

Equus

Oxydactylus

Protoceras

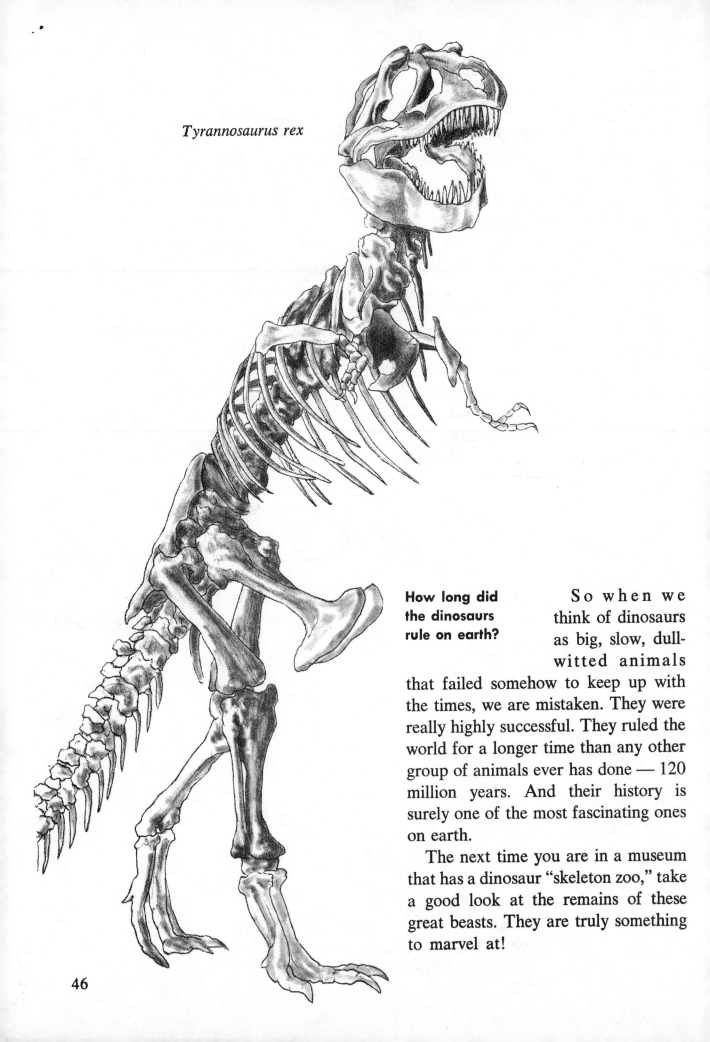

Tyrannosaurus rex

How long did the dinosaurs rule on earth?

So when we think of dinosaurs as big, slow, dull-witted animals that failed somehow to keep up with the times, we are mistaken. They were really highly successful. They ruled the world for a longer time than any other group of animals ever has done — 120 million years. And their history is surely one of the most fascinating ones on earth.

The next time you are in a museum that has a dinosaur "skeleton zoo," take a good look at the remains of these great beasts. They are truly something to marvel at!

How are mammals different from dinosaurs?

But where the dinosaurs had huge bodies and tiny brains, the mammals had smaller bodies and larger brains. The mammals were smarter and more active than the dinosaurs. And they were able to change more easily when the world changed.

While dinosaurs were cold-blooded, mammals are warm-blooded; dinosaurs laid eggs, but mammals give birth to living offspring; further, female mammals have milk glands and suckle their young.

So when the great dinosaurs died out, the little mammals had the world for themselves. They have grown and developed, and mammals have been ruling the world ever since.

We live in the Age of Mammals which started about 70 million years ago. Although that is a very long time, it is not nearly as long as the Age of Dinosaurs. Dinosaurs were the most important animals on earth for 120 million years.

SOME TYPICAL MAMMALS

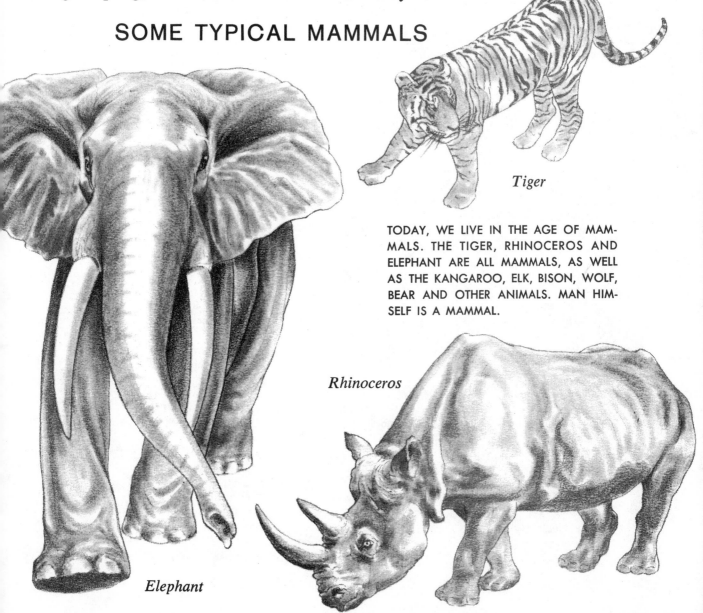

Tiger

TODAY, WE LIVE IN THE AGE OF MAMMALS. THE TIGER, RHINOCEROS AND ELEPHANT ARE ALL MAMMALS, AS WELL AS THE KANGAROO, ELK, BISON, WOLF, BEAR AND OTHER ANIMALS. MAN HIMSELF IS A MAMMAL.

Rhinoceros

Elephant

GLOSSARY OF DINOSAURS
AND OTHER PREHISTORIC ANIMALS

Prehistoric Animal	Phonetic Spelling	Derivation
Allosaurus	al-uh-SOR-us	other lizard
Amebelodon	am-eh-beh-LOH-don	shovel-tusk
Ankylosaurus	an-kil-uh-SOR-us	curved lizard
Archaeopteryx	ar-kee-OP-ter-iks	ancient wing
Archelon	AR-kee-lon	ruler tortoise
Barylambda	bare-ee-LAM-duh	heavy L (lamba: L)
Brachauchenius	brak-au-KEEN-ee-us	short-necked
Brachiosaurus	brak-ee-uh-SOR-us	arm lizard
Brontosaurus	bron-tuh-SOR-us	thunder lizard
Camptosaurus	kamp-tuh-SOR-us	bent lizard
Cheirolepis	ky-ROL-eh-pis	hand scale
Cladoselache	klay-duh-SEE-luh-kee	branched sea-fish
Dimetrodon	dye-MET-ruh-don	double-measure tooth
Dimorphodon	dye-MOR-fuh-don	two-forms tooth
Dinichthys	dye-NIK-this	terrible fish
Diplodocus	dih-PLOD-uh-kuss	double beam
Dolichosoma	doll-ee-kuh-SO-muh	long body
Elasmosaurus	ee-lass-moh-SOR-us	plated lizard
Eohippus	ee-oh-HIP-us	dawn horse
Equus	EE-kwuss	horse
Eurhinosaurus	yoor-rine-uh-SOR-us	large-snout lizard
Hoplopteryx	hop-LOP-ter-iks	armored wing
Ichthyosaurus	ik-thee-uh-SOR-us	fish-lizard
Iguanodon	ih-GWAN-uh-don	iquana lizard tooth
Indricotherium	in-drik-uh-THEE-ree-um	Indrico beast
Kannemeyeria	kan-eh-MY-ree-uh	(after Dr. Kannemeyer)
Mosasaurus	mo-suh-SOR-us	Meuse lizard (from Meuse R., Belg.)
Ornithopoda	or-nee-THOP-uh-duh	bird foot
Oxydactylus	ock-see-DAK-till-us	sharp finger
Patriofelis	pat-ree-oh-FEE-liss	ancestral cat
Phytosaur	FY-tuh-sor	plant lizard
Plesiosaurus	plees-ee-uh-SOR-us	near lizard
Pleuracanthus	ploo-ruh-CAN-this	rib spine
Podokesaurus	poh-dok-eh-SOR-us	swift-footed lizard
Portheus	por-THEE-us	(from) to destroy
Protoceras	pro-TAH-ser-iss	first horn
Protoceratops	proh-toh-SER-uh-tops	first horn-face
Pteranodon	ter-AN-uh-don	toothless wing
Rhamphorhynchus	ram-fuh-RINK-us	prow beak
Saltoposuchus	sal-tuh-puh-SOOK-us	(derivation unknown)
Seymouria	see-MOOR-ee-uh	Seymour (town in Texas)
Smilodon	SMY-luh-don	carving-knife tooth
Stegosaurus	steg-uh-SOR-us	cover lizard
Styracosaurus	sty-rack-uh-SOR-us	spike lizard
Titanothere	ty-TAY-nuth-heer	Titan beast
Trachodon	TRAK-uh-don	rough-toothed
Triceratops	try-SER-uh-tops	three-horned face
Tylosaurus	tie-loh-SOR-us	knot-lizard
Tyrannosaurus rex	ty-ran-uh-SOR-us rex	king of the tyrant lizards
Uintatherium	yoo-in-tuh-THEE-ree-um	Uinta beast (Uinta Cty., Wyo.)
Varanops	vuh-RAN-ops	lizard-like